Job Interview Body Language

Win the Job with "S-I-M-P-L-E Strategies"

Michael J. Willson and Karen Kelly

San Jose, California

ISBN 978-0-615-28918-2

Printed in the United States of America.

Dedications

KAREN KELLY

To my husband, Ed, and the rest of my family, thanks for always believing in me. Even when you thought I was nuts.

– Karen Kelly

MICHAEL J. WILLSON

To my wife Patti, thank you for continuing to make my life exciting, spontaneous and eventful. To my children, Matthew, Jennifer and Tiffany, each of you bring special meaning into my life. My world would be empty without all of you.

– Michael Willson

Win the Job with "S-I-M-P-L-E Strategies"

Acknowledgments

We would like to express our deep appreciation to those who have contributed to the success of our book:

To Cheryl Phelps, thank you for your invaluable editing assistance. Your gracious help gave us the means to keep our words and ideas moving forward and with a true direction.

To Sara Aurich, Jenny Fernando, Charlie Martin, Lin McJunkin, Elizabeth Pate-Morton, Patti Lovetro-Clarke, Cheryl Phelps and Lizz Pellett, your insightful and poignant stories added flavor and humor to our topics.

To Patti Willson, Eleze Armstrong and Jennifer Harrop-Willson, thank you for spending your time and effort in reading our rough drafts, offering input, and giving us encouragement. Your help made our writing flow in a dramatically better fashion.

Thank you to the following people for allowing us to use their images inside our book: Ed McJay, Polina Bernstein, Jennifer Harrop-Willson, Matthew Phillips, Brittany Welby, Tiffany Willson, Anandi Martinez and Patti Willson.

Table of Contents

Introduction

"Build success by building a successful image through the use of body language." –Willson-Kelly

Many people are finding themselves out of work and struggling to find a decent job. The competition for new jobs is fierce. To win a coveted position, the job seeker has to be a stand out – a real *star*. They not only have to have the right education, qualifications, and experience, but also that "something extra" that will set them apart.

What about you? Have you got that something extra? Are you doing everything within your power to make yourself the most attractive and sought-after job applicant?

Several studies have suggested that body language or body gestures may account for 60% to 80% of all your communications. What you say and the way you say it is important, but the true meanings behind your words may be revealed in the way you hold your body or through the use of gestures and facial expressions. This book is dedicated to helping you understand how to use these non-verbal communication skills to your advantage.

Through *Job Interview Body Language – Win the Job with "S-I-M-P-L-E Strategies"*, we're going to help you make all the right moves. We're going to teach you what to wear, how to sit, where to place your hands, how to perfect your smile, and other positive gestures that will give you an advantage.

We'll also identify which gestures may give the wrong impression and should be avoided. We're going to prepare you to perform the perfect job interview so you can elbow out the competition and win the job!

Our S-I-M-P-L-E acronym will serve as a quick reminder of what's important as you prepare for the big interview. Concentrating on these SIMPLE steps will make you stand out from all the other job applicants. Armed with a killer corporate style and incredibly effective body language skills, there will be no stopping you. Let's review our SIMPLE steps.

S tyle

In Chapters 1 and 2, we'll talk about the importance of having the right look, wearing the right clothes, makeup, jewelry, and more. Dressing like you're already a success is great, but did you know that over dressing could cost you the job?

I nterpreting Body Signals

In Chapters 3, 4, and 5, we'll discuss the importance of using effective body language skills. It will be important for you to send positive information to your interviewer via your own body language, however, you will gain great insight by understanding how to interpret the body language of your interviewer.

M orale

Chapters 6 and 7, we show you how to project a confident and upbeat image (even if you're not feeling it at the moment) by using simple body language skills and positive affirmations (a tried and true confidence builder).

P reparations

In Chapters 8 and 9, we want to show you how to be prepared for every eventuality. Being prepared can do
wonders for your confidence level. But what if things
aren't going the way you'd like? Well, we can help you
turn things around with some easy body language tricks
and tips.

L istening

In Chapter 10, we'll teach you how to listen for the verbal clues that may tell you how well you performed
during the interview. Remember, words alone don't tell
the whole story, so we'll also look at how to read your
interviewer's non-verbal clues.

E xit

In Chapter 11, we'll teach you how to make a fantastic
exit, putting a perfect ending to the perfect interview.

Willson-Kelly Presentations

Win the Job with "S-I-M-P-L-E Strategies"

1

FIRST APPEARANCE

Making a good first impression is important in any situation. But it's especially important at a job interview. This is where you begin to set the tone for the rest of your interview. Your personal features, the way you're dressed, and how you're groomed all play significant parts in creating a good first impression.

Making a great first impression is a good idea, but what if you don't? Can this ruin all your chances for the job? If you make a slight error or mistake at the beginning of an interview, all is not lost. Many people try so hard to make a great first impression, that if anything goes wrong, they lose confidence and don't present themselves well during the remainder of the interview. Fortunately, a bad first impression can be overturned or corrected during the interview process. Since the interview is where you sell yourself and present your ability to fulfill the position, why not help yourself by spending the extra time and effort in making a fantastic first impression?

First impressions happen within the first several seconds of meeting someone new. Many studies show that it can happen in as little as seven seconds. With such a small window of opportunity, you've got to make every second count. Before the questioning even begins, your interviewer is making judgments about you based upon your personal appearance. They begin to wonder: Are you friendly? Are you affable or arrogant? How well do you interact with others? Do you pay attention to details and are you a good candidate for the position? Since your personal appearance is under such scrutiny, let's start by focusing on how to create a look that tells your interviewer you're a winner.

S-I-M-P-L-E Strategies in Action

"Boy, THAT Made an Impression!" –
Submitted by Elizabeth Pate-Morton

My absolute favorite interview was at my last company. I was interviewing a candidate and the entire time we were talking I couldn't help but notice that his zipper was down and his white shirt was sticking out. Against black pants, that would be pretty hard not to notice! As we wrapped it up, I wanted to be sure I didn't embarrass him but also didn't want him going to the next person with his "Security Breach at Pant-aloni Island" going on. So as he stood up I mentioned politely that his zipper was down. He turned around so that his back was to me and hunched over to pull up the zipper - just as the executive of the department he was applying to was walking by. He looks at me with a "what the heck?!" look. I just tossed my hands up like "Wasn't me!" The candidate missed it all since he was so focused on his zipper. We actually hired him and he was awesome!

Grooming

One unfortunate truth of our society is that good-looking people get an advantage over those less attractive. Studies show that attractive people are often assumed to possess a number of positive social traits as well as greater intelligence. This assumption can influence your interviewer, so why not do everything you can to make yourself more attractive? Pay attention to details. Good grooming is essential, so let's start at the top.

HAIR: It's important that your hair be cut and styled appropriately for the business setting. Men, be sure that neck hair, ear hair, and wild eyebrow hair is removed. Be careful about getting a new haircut or hairstyle right before the interview. Even your "regular" cut needs a few days to calm down and lay right. Women with long hair should consider a style that pulls hair up and away from the face. Casting agents tell us they will pick the actor whose face, chin, and neck are seen clearly in a headshot versus the actor whose features are covered by hair, bangs, or whiskers.

Wearing long hair in loose waves or curls may send the wrong message. Long flowing hair is perceived as being more sexy or sensuous and may be distracting in the work place. Even shorter styles need to be kept neat and clean with hair being kept out of the face and eyes.

With all the wonderful products available, there is absolutely no excuse for having dandruff. Make certain to check your shoulders, eyebrows, and even your eye glasses in a mirror just before entering the office for your interview. Then, no scratching! One quick scratch can lead to more flakes. If you're wearing a dark shirt or jacket, be extra careful about controlling dandruff.

WK *A S-I-M-P-L-E Idea:*

You will find many excellent products for combating dandruff on the shelves of your local grocery and/or drug stores. They clean and condition your hair and leave your scalp and shoulders flake free. If you're on a tight budget, you can purchase these shampoos at your favorite buy-in-bulk superstores.

Both men and women need to be conservative when it comes to hair color. It's fine to have your hair professionally colored or highlighted (or do it yourself if you're skilled), but wild colors and outrageous styles are definitely inappropriate. Save the pink highlights and hair glitter for your personal life.

TEETH/BREATH: White teeth and fresh breath are always appreciated. A gorgeous smile with sparkling white teeth will make you appear more youthful, attractive, and likeable. Take a moment to look in a mirror and see how your teeth look. Age, smoking, and coffee drinking can yellow teeth over time. There are many affordable products on the market that can dramatically improve the appearance of your teeth and help refresh your breath. You will be judged on your smile, so make it sparkle, and don't forget to use a breath freshener just before you step in for your interview.

HANDS/FINGERNAILS: Your hands are always visible. Have your fingernails trimmed, cleaned, and/or polished. Dirty fingernails will create a distasteful distraction for your interviewer and can point out your lack of attention to detail. Women should avoid excessively long nails, especially when applying for a job that requires computer work. Potential employers may wonder if your nails will interfere with your work.

Select a nail polish color that is soft and muted or consider skipping polish altogether.

TATTOOS/PIERCINGS: Piercings and tattoos have become very popular but are still considered a negative in the business environment. Piercing of the nose, lips, eyebrows, or excessive piercings of the ears can have a detrimental effect in your negotiations and can be considered unprofessional for certain positions. We recommend that you always remove these types of piercings before your interview (this includes men).

That snake tattoo may have impressed your friends after a couple of drinks, but most likely won't impress a Fortune 500 company recruiter. Covering up your body art with clothing or special makeup can prove to be a wise decision.

WK *A S-I-M-P-L-E Idea:*

There is a special makeup called Derma Blend used for covering scars, birthmarks, etc. which can be found at your local drugstore. It's great for temporarily covering a tattoo for a job interview. It's waterproof but washes off easily with soap and water when no longer needed.

MAKEUP: For women, the use of makeup needs to be carefully thought out. The sparkly makeup you wear to a nightclub might not be the appropriate look for your job interview. Apply makeup lightly and keep it looking natural. Taupes, tawny browns, and neutral grays are good eye shadow colors, and soft pinks, corals, peaches, and other warm skin tones are good for lipstick choices.

We do not suggest going without makeup. Not wearing makeup may cause others to perceive you as being less attractive or even possibly less intelligent. Natural looking makeup, shiny hair, simple jewelry and a tailored suit will convey confidence, beauty, and intelligence – the whole package. The care you give your personal appearance will speak volumes to your interviewer and dressing just a little bit better than all the other candidates will set you apart and could help you land the job.

PERFUMES/AFTERSHAVES: We all like to smell good, but over-use of fragrance can be a turn off for your interviewer. Like your accessories, perfumes should enhance and not overpower. Too much scent may give off the wrong signal and end your interview before it even starts. Some people are hyper sensitive to fragrances. It would not bode well for your interviewer to suffer an allergic reaction to your fragrance. When in doubt, it would be best to use fragrances sparingly or perhaps skip perfumes and colognes altogether.

Prior to the Interview

Now that you're groomed and looking like a winner, it's time to enter the office building for your interview. Always be kind and polite to the receptionist. You never know who he or she has as a friend. If the receptionist has a regular lunch date with your interviewer, you definitely want him or her on your side. Never make assumptions and work to convince everyone you are the right person for the job.

A S-I-M-P-L-E Idea:

To help calm your nerves and loosen up your speaking skills, we find that opening a conversation with the receptionist while you wait, can help. It takes your mind off the impending interview which can lessen your anxiety and gives you a congenial appearance - a great look for the recruiter to see when they come to retrieve you for your interview.

After you check-in, take a seat and sit up straight while you wait. Try not to cross your legs, keep both feet flat on the floor, with arms at your side or folded comfortably in your lap. Don't chew gum, play with your keys, tap your feet, or use your cell phone. In fact, it's better to leave your cell phone in the car. You certainly don't want it to ring during your interview, especially if you use special tones. Having an obnoxious ring-tone playing as you respond to the interviewer's questions will not only be embarrassing, but it may eliminate you from the competition.

Summary

Things to review prior to your job interview:

- Style or cut your hair
- Check dandruff
- Remove wild hairs
- Consider whitening teeth
- Use a breath freshener
- Trim, clean, and/or polish fingernails
- Cover tattoos

Summary *(Continued)*

- Remove excessive piercings
- Wear light, natural makeup
- Use colognes and fragrances lightly, or skip altogether
- No cell phones
- Don't fidget
- Treat *everyone* as a decision maker

2

WINNING ATTIRE

Anywhere and everywhere you go, the first thing people will notice about you is your personal appearance. Being creative, expressive, and daring are wonderful traits to possess, but being too unconventional in your personal style may actually work against you in the job market. If you're really serious about getting the job, leave your flashy stuff at home and wear something appropriate and understated to the interview.

Now notice: we said "understated", not "underdressed". In other words, if you're interviewing for a pizza delivery position, wearing jeans and sneakers might be fine. However, you would be dreadfully *underdressed* interviewing for a corporate office position. OK, we know you *know* this. But did you know that "overdressing" could cost you the job as well? Got your attention?

Out dressing the boss or other management and employees, may send the message that you don't really need the job. Being overdressed could be perceived by some as being smug and pretentious. Others may feel you care more about your look or style than you do about the job. You want to show your interviewer respect by dressing appropriately for the occasion, but strive for some balance.

Proper Attire

Obviously the business suit is a perfect choice for most corporate positions. This is true for both men and women. It would be wise to avoid wearing miniskirts, tight sweaters, or outfits that have holes or stains. Women can avoid looking too masculine by wearing a business suit tailored to show off the waistline, some soft details, and more feminine colors. If in doubt, a well-cut suit in neutral tones such as black, blue, tan or gray is ideal.

WK *A S-I-M-P-L-E Idea:*

If your budget is tight, opt for a less expensive suit and spend just a little more to have it altered so that it fits you perfectly. It is the perfect fit, and not the actual garment, that will make you look like you're wearing a fine piece of clothing.

A man's suit should also be tailored to accentuate wide shoulders and a tapered waist. Wearing tailored clothes that show your feminine or masculine shape make you look fit, healthy, and more attractive. Many of us take heroic measures to cover up our shapes, particularly if we're carrying around a few extra pounds. But wearing loose, shapeless clothing will not be in your best interest. It's a sad fact that overweight people make less money than their thinner counterparts. If you're overweight, give yourself an advantage and have your clothes tailored to fit perfectly in the shoulders, sleeve length, waist, pant/skirt length, and make sure there are no strains on buttons or fabric.

Color and Personal Style

As mentioned above, wearing a business suit to a corporate interview is ideal. However, some of you, women in particular, wouldn't be caught dead in a business suit and we know it. Does this mean you're out of the running for a corporate position? No, of course it doesn't. But you will need to be cautious about the attire you choose to wear to your interview. Our advice is designed to help you fit in, look like a team member, and allow your qualifications, training, and education to take center stage at your job interview. You don't want to be overshadowed by your own wardrobe. But, we think it's okay to be a little unique and still maintain a professional image.

If you refuse to wear a suit, women can opt for a straight skirt with nice lines (not too short), and a belted sweater or jacket (to emphasize the waistline) in the neutral tones we discussed before. You can liven up the look with a colorful blouse and nice accessories. Pair your ensemble with attractive shoes and a stylish purse and you will bypass the need to wear a suit yet still maintain a polished and professional image.

Men who are applying for corporate or office jobs have fewer clothing options than women. If you're applying for a job where the men in the company wear suits, you'd be best advised to hang in there and wear the suit.

For the most part, both men and women will want to keep accent colors mild and understated. If you just can't resist, add bold colors in small doses. For example, women can wear a brightly colored scarf, and men can opt for a tie in a bold color or pattern to make a statement.

If you'd like to be a little more daring about wearing colors, but you're unsure about what will compliment your skin tone, hair color, and eyes, you probably already own something in a color that's perfect for you. If people compliment you every time you wear that pale blue shirt, pay attention! Pale blue seems to be a good color for you, so select other clothing items or accessory pieces in pale blue. There are dozens of online sites that can help you determine your best color choices and if you need help putting an outfit together, visit your local department store and speak with their image consultant.

Though it might be preferable to wear the traditional business suit, you just may be unwilling or unable to do so. Whatever you decide to wear, be sure that it makes you feel and look good, and that it's appropriate to the job for which you're applying. Wearing clothes that make you feel good about yourself will give you added confidence which will be reflected in your positive body language. Positive body language may play an even bigger role in impressing your interviewer than the clothes you're wearing.

Personal Colors

Though it's impossible to tell you what colors would be perfect for your personal wardrobe, what follows are some basic guidelines that will help you determine what colors may flatter your own hair color, eye color, and skin tone. For more personalized information, you may wish to have your colors done by a professional color consultant and, of course, there are countless books and online sites devoted to this very subject.

BRUNETTES: Brunettes look lovely in jewel tones - think turquoise, sapphire blues, and ruby reds. Purple, cranberry red, lime and mint green are other excellent choices, as well as pink, peach, and certain tans. Many brunettes look great in black, but if it's too severe, consider a gray or navy. Yellow is a difficult color for brunettes to wear and even other colors may have yellow undertones. You'll have to decide what works best for you based on your own skin color.

BLONDES: If you're blonde, look for clothing colors in soft pastels. Baby pink and blue, as well as an icy blue works nicely on pale-skinned, blue-eyed blondes. Other wonderful color choices include soft ivory, apricot, and peach. Blondes can also wear champagne, pale yellow, and cream. The exception to the pastel rule may be a rich, ruby red. Many blondes can wear red with beautiful results.

REDHEADS: Redheads look brilliant in fall colors. Pumpkin, spicy orange, mossy or olive green compliments red hair beautifully. Redheads can often wear yellows and golds, but again, this may depend on your own personal coloring and skin tone. If your skin isn't too ruddy, pink might be a fabulous color choice. Emerald green, dark purple, and deep lilac are other excellent options.

BLACK HAIR: If you have black hair, you may find that pure white, true red, and brilliant blue are exciting color choices that will dramatically show off your dark hair color. Bright lemon-yellow, hot pink and royal blue are other bold choices that blondes, brunettes, and redheads may not be able to wear. These lively colors are perfect with gorgeous black hair.

GRAY HAIR: If you have gray hair, you may be able to wear just about any color you like. If selecting a pastel, be careful that the color doesn't wash you out too much. Grays look beautiful in plums, purples, mauves, and any other pink hues, especially pinks with bluish undertones. Grays can also wear ivory, apricot, coral, and deep, rich reds. Most grays look fabulous in black, charcoal, and navy.

S-I-M-P-L-E Strategies in Action

"Clothes and Confidence" — *Submitted by Sara Aurich*

My only set of formal interviews occurred many years ago, shortly after I graduated from college. Having the right outfit gave me confidence. My tailored navy blue suit, white silk blouse, subtle jewelry and practical yet stylish shoes said, "I'm one of you. I take myself and my job seriously. I am organized and detail oriented. I am respectful and I command respect. I will fit in with your other employees and make a good impression on your clients." It was the most expensive outfit I'd ever owned and I'd made a special trip from San Jose to an upscale department store in Palo Alto to purchase it. Wearing this outfit gave me confidence and calmed me down when I met with them. Already looking like what I was aspiring towards set the tone for confident body language.

Jewelry and Accessories

When deciding what accessories to wear, remember - less is better. Accessories should enhance your appearance and not be a distraction. A job interview is not the time to bring out all your *bling*. Choose carefully and select items that give a true reflection of your personality and are appropriate to the position for which you are applying.

Wearing an expensive designer watch to a job interview may be the right look for a corporate-executive position, but would be a bad choice if applying to stock the warehouse. A bit of an extreme example, but you get the idea. A few simple accessories are all you need to complete your look. Modest watches, plain rings, and small earrings work well.

WK *A S-I-M-P-L-E Idea:*

Eyeglasses, if you wear them, are an excellent accessory to wear when you want to appear more knowledgeable and intelligent - so much so, that if you don't need glasses, you may wish to purchase a pair with clear lenses.

Shoes

Remember, you're always being judged and evaluated, even *before* the interview starts. While waiting in the reception area, stand tall and use good posture. Tall people, just like good-looking people, get an advantage, so emphasize your height. Women, especially shorter women, should wear shoes with a heel – no spikes, stilettos or sandals – that would be appropriate for the office.

 Men, if you need a little extra height, consider using a lift or choose a shoe style that has a taller heel. If you bought shoes especially for the interview, test them out beforehand. This is not the time to find out you're not able to walk well or your new shoes hurt your feet. It's hard to be confident and poised while your feet are in pain.

Make sure the shoes you wear look good both coming and going. You don't want to end a great interview by turning around to leave and exposing worn and scuffed heels. Shoes need to be in good condition and well shined. Also, make sure your purse and/or briefcase is in good condition.

Other Considerations

If you're applying for a job where a uniform would be worn, it might be a good idea to wear something with a similar appearance for your interview. For example, if you're interviewing for a package delivery service and the uniform is a pair of brown pants and a brown shirt, you may want to wear brown slacks and a brown jacket. Dressing similarly to the uniform will give you the appearance of already being part of the team.

If you have knowledge beforehand about a dress code favored by the company's management and their employees, you may be ahead of the game. Again, dressing like you're already a part of the team will work to your advantage. You will seem like a good fit and part of the family.

Remember, you build success by building a successful image. Since your outer appearance is the first thing others will see, it's critical to present a professional, respectful, and appropriate image at your job interview.

Summary

Things to review prior to the job interview:

- Don't over dress or under dress
- Wear clothes that fit properly
- Ideal colors – black, blue, gray or tan
- Wear shoes that give extra height
- Accessorize sparingly
- Stand tall
- Dress appropriately for the position

3

THE GREETING

At this point, you're perfectly groomed and appropriately dressed and now you're seated in the reception area waiting for your opportunity to convince the interviewer that you're the best candidate for the job. You're about to make your first big impression and any mistakes at this time can put you at a disadvantage. As you're being called for the interview, stand and approach confidently. Make good eye contact with your interviewer. Have a smile on your face, extend your hand for a solid handshake, and make your greeting statement. Each one of these items is important, and if done correctly, will get your interview off to a good start.

All these specific elements need to come across smoothly and confidently. Let's review and discuss each of these maneuvers separately.

Your Walk

It's important to walk with confidence. Shuffling your feet or walking with your shoulders slumped and your head down will not give you an air of confidence. Work on holding your head and chest high. Try not to puff out your chest in an exaggerated way because, for men, this can be seen as a sign of arrogance or an act of intimidation. For women, it could bring unwanted attention and draw attention away from your overall appearance. Either of these attention getters can create the wrong impression.

It is best to stand tall with shoulders slightly back and arms resting comfortably at your sides. If you're holding a purse or briefcase, be sure to hold them in your left hand so you can shake hands with your right. Don't place or fold your arms in front of you as this creates a defensive barrier between you and the interviewer and gives the impression that you may be timid, shy, or hard to get to know.

WK *A S-I-M-P-L-E Idea:*

Here's a great way to perfect your posture. Stand in front of a mirror and position yourself with your back against a wall. Your heels, butt, and shoulders should make contact with the wall. This is proper posture alignment. Now, close your eyes and take a step away from the wall. This will help ingrain the feel of correct posture into your memory. Open your eyes and look in the mirror - see how others will observe you when you stand confidently. Practice this exercise at least once a day until it becomes second nature. Also practice your posture in different outfits to make sure your posture doesn't change if you're wearing a tie or jacket, for example.

Smile

Your smile can have a great influence upon the receiver and can actually give you an advantage. This is called the *"smile leniency effect"* and research shows that when you smile, you are judged to be a more sincere, sociable, and competent person when compared to a non-smiling individual.

Smiles need to be genuine. Most of us can easily identify a fake smile, and a fake smile does not create the same positive emotions. For examples of a "fake" smile, take a good look at your photo albums. Forced smiles never have the same impact as sincere smiles and are a major reason most people don't like the way they look in their photos.

Fake Smile

Genuine Smile

To give your best smile, you must use the entire face. A smile begins in the eyes. A genuine smile will crinkle the skin around the eyes (crow's feet). The cheeks will be slightly lifted and the person's teeth are fully exposed. A fake smile uses only the muscles around the mouth.

WK *A S-I-M-P-L-E Idea:*

While looking in a mirror, use a piece of paper to cover your mouth. Now smile. With your mouth covered, can you tell if you're smiling? If not, keep practicing until you can. The key, as we stated earlier, is engaging your eyes in your smile.

Good Eye Contact

Good eye contact is one of the most important tools you can use in building rapport with others. Looking someone directly in the eyes shows respect and interest in what they're saying. Good eye contact entails using what is called the *business gaze*. When using the business gaze your eyes rotate around a triangle on the face. This triangle goes from the center of the forehead and then from eye to eye. Maintaining this type of eye contact is desirable and appropriate in a business setting.

WK *A S-I-M-P-L-E Idea:*

Try this easy trick: when you first meet your interviewer, try to identify the color of their eyes. This simple process will help you increase your eye contact with the interviewer immediately.

Staring at just one area of the face can be unsettling and can give you the appearance of being a predator. It's better to move your eyes around the business-gaze triangle which will seem more natural and unthreatening. Avoid darting your eyes around quickly as this will lose the beneficial effect.

Good eye contact conveys your interest in what the other person is saying and lets the speaker know that their message or content is being received. Though you may want to take notes during an interview, writing while the other person speaks can be detrimental. Notice how you feel when people don't maintain eye contact with you as you speak. Poor or decreased eye contact gives the impression of arrogance or loss of interest. Definitely not the signals you want to send.

S-I-M-P-L-E Strategies in Action

"Do You Feel Lucky?" — *Submitted by Charlie Martin*

The applicant was not particularly attentive and seldom made eye contact until which time I completed my discussion regarding handguns. At this point, the prospective employee, without turning his head to face me, shifted his eyes toward me and inquired in a monotone voice "When do I get a gun?" After briefly explaining once again that the permitting of handguns by security personnel was based on many factors, I quickly concluded the interview and escorted the now "non-prospective" employee off the premises.

Initiate a Handshake

We recommend holding a purse or briefcase in your left hand, so your right hand can be extended to initiate a proper and solid handshake.

Shaking hands is a simple process, but there are several elements of this ritual that can make or break your good first impression. For example, grabbing and squeezing the interviewer's hand too tightly (or worse, only grabbing their fingertips) and squeezing hard, sends a very negative message. Squeezing too hard can cause pain to the interviewer and may be seen as a sign of dominance.

Proper Handshake

Just as squeezing too hard sends the wrong message, not using enough pressure comes off as weak, timid, and insecure. Your best bet is to try and mirror the same amount of pressure the interviewer is sending back to you.

Grasping their hand with both of your hands can seem like you're trying too hard to be accepted. A two-handed handshake is too personal and not appropriate in business settings. A proper handshake begins by keeping your thumb up and pointed toward the ceiling. The interviewer's palm should fit easily into your palm. Keep your thumb and theirs pointing up, as this will help create equality between the both of you. Bend your arm at the elbow since shaking hands with a straight or locked arm can make it look as though you want to create distance between you and the receiver. A solid grip with two or three firm shakes is all you need.

WK *A S-I-M-P-L-E Idea:*

Women in business need to be particularly careful about their handshakes. Men have had centuries of perfecting their handshakes, but women still struggle with this traditionally male ritual. If necessary, practice with a friend until you can give a good, confident handshake.

Interpreting Handshakes

How the interviewer presents their handshake can give you insights into their personality and can give you an advantage in the interview process.

DOMINANT HANDSHAKE: Anyone who uses a dominant handshake, where their palm is facing down causing you to shake hands with your palm facing up, is someone who has low self-esteem and feels they need to be in control. Use this to your benefit and allow them to feel they're in complete control during the interview. You'll still work at selling your abilities to meet the requirements for the job, but letting them "lead" will bolster their ego, and you'll be viewed as a cooperative and potential prospect.

THE VICE GRIP: Unlike the dominant handshake, the other person's hand is in the neutral position, but they feel a need to try to crush your hand. As with the dominant handshake, the vice grip is all about ego, but since their hand was in the neutral position, they may be offering a level playing field. Tread lightly in the beginning until you have an understanding of how level the playing field may be.

LIMP HANDED: This type of a handshake is a sign of weakness and could lead to a boring or stagnant interview. This person is not a leader and may have difficulty conducting an effective interview. You'll have to take a more active role in the process. You may even need to lead the interview. Again use this to your advantage and lead the interview into areas that best describe your finest assets.

MAKING CORRECTIONS: Depending upon the situation, you may feel you need to correct the interviewer's handshake. If you're interviewing for a position that requires leadership and an assertive personality, it may be in your best interest to correct the dominant handshake. This can be done easily by clasping their hand with both of yours, tilt your head back slightly as you continue to look them straight in the eyes. Now adjust their hand by turning it into the neutral position while you thank them for taking the time to meet with you. It's important to make this statement while you're still making hand contact. It'll help divert their attention from the adjustments you're making, but on a subconscious level, your point will have been made.

This is a powerful maneuver that when used in the wrong situation can backfire, so use considerable discretion.

WK *A S-I-M-P-L-E Idea:*

Sweaty Palms – Try carrying a napkin or handkerchief in your pocket. Dry your hands discreetly in your pocket before shaking hands. Another option for those who have chronic wet palms (hyperhidrosis) is to apply an unscented, aluminum salt-based "antiperspirant" to your hands prior to any meetings.

Greeting Statement

Start off the interview by giving a simple but strong statement, such as thanking your interviewer for seeing you. Again if possible, begin this statement before releasing the person's hand from the handshake. Statements made while you still have contact will have more of a positive impact. Repeating the interviewer's name adds more emphasis to your statement.

If you can manage it, try not to look down as you end your statement or handshake. It's difficult to maintain eye contact with someone you've just met, but eye contact continues to establish the positive connection you're making and diverting your eyes will break this bond. Looking away nervously is a sign of submissiveness and should be avoided. Speaking, shaking hands, and making proper eye contact may be skills you need to practice, but they will be well worth the effort. By perfecting these skills, you will be seen as confident, intelligent and very likeable in the process. These are all qualities that any company would value in its employees, so put in the work.

Summary

Things to do for a proper greeting:

- Walk confidently
- Use a genuine smile
- Make and maintain good eye contact
- Initiate a proper handshake
- Make a statement of gratitude for your interviewer's time

4

KEYS TO BEING LIKED

You've made it inside, and you're about to begin the interview process. You've done your homework, rehearsed all your stories, and taken stock of your career. Now is the time to establish a great rapport with your interviewer. Your main goal, other than thoroughly describing how your skills and abilities are perfect for the job, is to get the interviewer to *like* you. People who are not well liked during the interview process are rarely hired for the position. People want to work with others they find interesting, confident, and well respected. To help establish great rapport, consider using the following body language skills or techniques during your interview.

Mirroring

Have you ever noticed a couple who's in love? They appear to be a reflection of each other in the way they hold their bodies, the positions of their hands and arms, and the direction of their feet. This matching of each other's body language shows an intimate rapport. They may not even realize what's happening.

The process of being in sync with another person is what we call mirroring or pacing.

When someone mimics or mirrors our gestures and body positions, our subconscious mind finds these actions soothing and comfortable. It gives the impression that we are looking into a mirror, and we like what we see.

If done correctly, mirroring your interviewer during the interview process can give you a strong advantage. It's a simple and basic form of establishing friendship and rapport.

Start your interview by sitting in a neutral position. Watch the movements and body positions of your interviewer. Slowly, over a period of time, begin to adjust your core body angle to be in sync with theirs. Next, begin to move the rest of your body. First, move your legs and then your arms. Finally, you should end up in almost the same position as your interviewer.

If the interviewer moves into another position, subtly alter yours. Be careful not to change your positions too abruptly. Being obvious about this may end up embarrassing both you and your interviewer. Simply wait a few seconds before moving into that reflective position.

Once you think you have established the connection, you may want to test it to confirm that the bond has been made. This is simply done by moving into a different position. Move your arm or leg into a slightly different angle. We strongly suggest that you do not move your chest or re-orient your body position. Changing your core body position can actually break the connection or show a change in attitude. It may take a few moments, but if your interviewer eventually responds by moving into the same position, you have now established rapport and increased the likelihood that this person finds you interesting and likeable.

Active Gestures

Sitting motionless and not moving anything but your mouth gives you the appearance of being uptight, stiff, and unapproachable. Using casual arm and hand gestures will show you as an open and enthusiastic person. Be careful though, and keep your gestures small. A good rule-of-thumb is to keep your arm and hand gestures within the core area of your body. Try not to extend your gestures beyond the width of your shoulders. Palms up and hands open are universally accepted as friendly, non-threatening gestures. Clenched fists, arms behind your back, hands hidden inside your pockets, or folding your arms across your chest may lead the interviewer to believe that you have a closed mind, you're insecure, and possibly angry. It can also give the impression you're trying to hide something, so keep your hands in view at all times.

Over-gesturing can have a negative effect. Wild arm movements and big, sweeping gestures are used to draw attention to ourselves. Unfortunately, in certain situations, that attention may be negative. Large gestures can make you look flighty, foolish, and out of control. This can create too many questions about your personality and bring into doubt your ability to be part of the team.

Wild Gestures

29

S-I-M-P-L-E *Strategies in Action*

"Salsa Dancing" — *Submitted by Elizabeth Pate-Morton*

I was interviewing a guy a few years ago for a position in Finance. He was well qualified and seemed like a genuinely nice guy and I was quite interested in him as a serious candidate to consider....until he announced to me that he wasn't just some "boring Finance guy" and that he "really knew how to have fun" and at that point, he jumped up out of the chair and started Salsa Dancing around my office to show me how "fun" he was. That body language didn't work so well for him.

A positive gesture, however, is the head nod. Use the head nod when others are speaking to indicate interest and agreement. Be careful not to nod too fast, since that may indicate impatience, but rather nod your head slowly. It demonstrates you agree with them, without having to interrupt, and it also encourages the person to continue talking. The more a person talks, the more they feel important. It's a natural human reaction.

As important as it is to use positive and appropriate gestures, you'll need to be careful about using nervous body language, such as touching your face (eyes, nose, mouth) as these types of gestures often signal deceit, even though they may be innocent, nervous tics. Men should refrain from constant tie straightening or collar tugging as this too may make you look like you're hiding something and are scared of getting caught.

Women should keep their hands out of their hair (in Chapter 2 we suggested wearing long hair pulled up and off the face) and refrain from fluffing, flipping, or tucking hair behind the ears. When women touch their hair, particularly when speaking with a man, it is seen as a sign of romantic interest and would likely be viewed as flirting. This, of course, would be inappropriate for a job interview.

Body Angles

As with mirroring, the angle of your body speaks volumes to the other person, or in this case, your interviewer. Leaning back with your legs crossed with the ankle of one leg resting on the thigh of the other leg (most commonly used by men), is not an appealing body position. It can be interpreted as being too casual, uncaring, or even arrogant. Both men and women should sit upright with your chest facing directly at the person you're speaking with, your feet flat on the floor, and leaning forward slightly. This position says you're confident and ready to begin the interview process. It also encourages more verbal interaction. Angling your chest off to the side or rolling your shoulders forward is an avoidance gesture and a sign of insecurity. This positioning would not convey the confident image you're hoping to exhibit.

Refrain from crossing anything. Crossing your hands, arms, or legs may be viewed or perceived as a sign of defensiveness. If accompanied by a shoulder roll, these actions will give you a look of submissiveness.

Your feet need to be flat on the floor (unless you are mirroring the interviewer) and pointed toward the person with whom you're speaking. The farther away from your brain a body part is located (such as legs and feet), the more difficult it is to consciously control that part of your body. As a result, those body parts may signal our true desires and feelings. Unfortunately, we may not wish to have those feelings known to others, so we need to be mindful of what our body language may be saying when we're not aware.

31

For example, if you were having a conversation with someone and you found them boring, you might notice that your feet were pointing toward the nearest exit, mimicking your internal desire to move away from that person - just the same way your feet may point to the person you find the most interesting or enjoyable if you were at a party or social gathering.

Controlling the body language of your legs and feet may be more challenging, but worth the effort, especially if you're trying to keep from sending unwanted information to your interviewer.

Remove Barriers

Do not use your arms or other items to create a divide between you and the interviewer. Holding a briefcase on your lap or clutching it against your chest creates a barrier. This barrier is clearly seen and easily felt during the interview process.

Remove Barriers

Place your purse or briefcase on the ground next to you. Refrain from holding anything in your hands as well. A pen or tablet of paper can interfere with you being able to make certain gestures and can become a distraction to the interviewer. Holding a pen and clicking it repeatedly will act like Morse Code sending a message that you're nervous, anxious and unsure of yourself. Since we often perform these nervous habits without even knowing it, it may be better not to hold a pen in your hand at all.

32

WK *A* **S-I-M-P-L-E** *Idea:*

If you need to make a note, ask the interviewer if you can have a moment to document the item and then place the pen back out of your immediate reach. If you're seated at a table, make sure your writing pad or pen does not create a barrier by being in between you and the interviewer.

Remember to mirror your interviewer's body position and angles and use appropriate gestures to communicate and emphasize your key points. Keeping barriers from interfering with the rapport you're building will help your interviewer develop genuine feelings of fondness for you. This may just give you that extra edge over the competition.

Summary

Keys to being liked:

- Mirror the person you're speaking with
- Use positive and open body gestures
- Do not fold your arms, legs, hands, or feet
- Use a head nod when listening
- No wild gestures
- Position your body directly at the interviewer
- Sit up straight, feet on the floor, and lean forward slightly
- Refrain from playing with items such as pens and paper during your interview
- Remove all barriers

5

FACIAL EXPRESSIONS

Your emotions, such as anxiety, nervousness, fear, and happiness are all clearly seen on your face at any given moment. If your interviewer greets you and sees anxiety, nervousness, or fear on your face, you are going to lose that critical opportunity to make a great first impression.

Be Aware of Your Expressions

It's wise to be aware of your facial expressions, especially in important situations like job interviews. Sometimes an innocent expression, such as a creased forehead with your eyebrows pinched together (as though in deep concentration) may be perceived as anger, grouchiness, or disapproval. Strive to keep your facial expressions pleasant and friendly at all times.

Rarely can you make a mistake by smiling. Smiles trigger mirror neurons in our brain that automatically make other people smile. Use this to your advantage and smile as much as you can without looking as though you belong in an institution. As we mentioned earlier, work on your smile so that it looks authentic.

Looking Down Your Nose

Your mother has no doubt at some point during your lifetime, told you to stand up straight. Correct posture will go a long way in making a good impression, but take care that you don't stand in such a way that it causes you to "look down your nose." This is usually perceived as a gesture of contempt or a sign that you feel the person you're speaking with is inferior. If your interviewer is much shorter than you, you may want to lean in somewhat as you shake hands, look them warmly in the eyes and smile. This should set the right tone and keep you from looking down at them in a way that's viewed as negative.

Many times glasses can give you the appearance of being intellectual. But if you use glasses to read, you'll need to remind yourself not to peer over the tops of them. This again will give you the appearance of looking down your nose or sitting in a position of judgment.

Many actors, who play judges, use this gesture to give them that specific appearance. You do not want to promote that look during your interview. If you need to use your glasses to make a note or read an item, make sure to remove them immediately so that you do not inadvertently peer over them as you continue to listen or begin to speak to the interviewer.

Pursed Lips

As mentioned above, pinched eyebrows can give the appearance of anger or disapproval. The same is true for pinched or pursed lips. If you use this expression while your interviewer is talking, she may take it as a sign that you are skeptical, doubtful, or disapproving. It is unlikely that pursed lips will ever be seen as anything other than a negative.

Pursed Lips

If you notice this expression on your interviewer's face as you're speaking, it could spell trouble. If you think she may be in doubt of your skill or unsure of your resume, for example, it would be appropriate to say something like "it seems there may be something bothering you about my resume. I'd be happy to answer any questions for you."

Try to keep from constantly licking your lips. Sometimes when we're nervous, our mouth and lips get dry, but anxiously licking your lips will make you look unsure, insecure, and perhaps even deceitful.

Another lip movement to avoid is the lip roll. Again, dry lips may make you want to roll your lips inward to try to wet them. But what the lip roll says to your interviewer is that you might not be telling the truth about something. This will bring doubt into your relationship and could possibly sour your interview.

WK *A S-I-M-P-L-E Idea:*

To help avoid lip licking or the lip roll, try using a lip balm just before you go in for your interview.

Head Tilt

When someone tilts their head to one side, as long as they continue to use good eye contact, it's a sign that they're listening intently and they're interested in what you're saying. A head tilt with no eye contact could indicate that they're bored and are losing interest in what you're saying.

Resting Head on Hands

Picture someone sitting across the desk from you. You're talking and they're listening and you notice that their elbow is on the desktop and their head or chin is propped in their hand. What message would you get from this posture? Boredom?

Would you be pleased to see that type of reaction? Of course not, and neither would your interviewer. Remember what we discussed earlier about positive listening gestures. Lean forward, tilt your head, nod, and smile.

**A Positive & Open
Sitting Position**

Summary

For good facial expressions remember to:

- Make good eye contact
- Continue to use a genuine smile
- Use a positive head nod when listening
- Lean forward to show interest
- Don't "look down your nose"
- Try not use too much lip movement
- Don't rest your head on anything

6

DISPLAY CONFIDENCE

Humans have a natural fear of failure. We all have a need to feel accepted and be perceived as intelligent and important individuals. This is why job interviews can be a very intimidating process.

At a job interview we must open ourselves to being judged and evaluated. A complete stranger will be making judgments about you, deciding if you're smart enough, skilled enough, competent enough, nice enough, or friendly enough to fill the position. Then if you're *not* offered the position, the message seems to be that you're *not* smart enough or skilled enough, etc. That can be demoralizing.

With that in the back of your mind, you may find it difficult to act confidently. But acting confidently can be the determining factor as to whether or not you will be offered the position. We must at least create an air of confidence, even if we are not actually feeling it. We all like confident people – confidence is an extremely attractive quality. Here are some of the gestures that will help you give that attractive appearance of confidence.

41

S-I-M-P-L-E Strategies in Action

"It's Hard to be Confident with No Pants!" –

Submitted by Jenny Fernando

During the summer of 2006, I was looking to relocate from Sacramento back to the San Francisco Bay Area. The only thing holding me back was getting a new job before I made the move. I conducted a job search and found a position I qualified for. I contacted the employer and scheduled an interview for the following Friday.

On Thursday, I drove into town. That evening, I decided to prepare my interview outfit by making sure my pants and blouse were ironed. I quickly found my blouse but discovered I had left my pants in Sacramento! Thinking fast, I made a trip to the nearest department store and found the perfect pair of pants. The only problem was, because I'm short, the pant legs draped at least 8 inches past my feet. I figured I would simply fold the bottoms up and use safety pins to keep the hem in place. Unfortunately, as I later discovered, I didn't have any safety pins either, so I had to hold up the hem of my pants with straight pins!

On the morning of the interview, my pants held together with straight pins, I left for my job interview. It didn't go well. I was fighting an attack of bronchitis, pins were poking me in the ankles, and I arrived an hour late due to traffic and getting lost. Not surprisingly, I didn't hear anything about the job. But two weeks later, I got a call. I was hired!

A Level Head

We have addressed your body posture earlier in this book. Good posture, whether you're standing or seated, will continue to be important throughout the interview. But let's discuss the importance of holding your head in positions that will give you the best advantage.

Your best bet is to keep your head in a neutral position. You can achieve this by positioning your chin on the same horizontal plane as the floor. Lifting your chin or leaning your head back gives the impression of arrogance. It's a dominant head position which may cause you to "look down your nose". This sends a bad or even hostile signal to your interviewer.

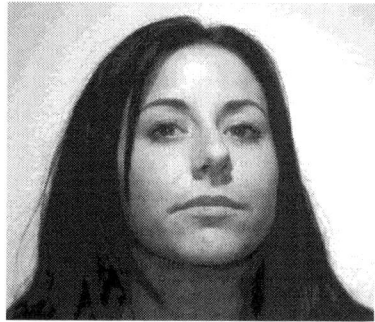

Negative Head Position

In the last chapter we said that leaning your head back and looking down your nose is not advised, but neither is dropping your head forward and lowering your chin. This position will give the impression of being submissive. Showing signs of submission, timidity, or shyness would only display a lack of confidence. Ducking your head will produce a similar effect. It's best not to lower your head or chin any time during the interview. Be aware and refrain from lowering your eyes, shoulders, or head during your meeting.

Your Voice

Your voice will also give clues as to your level of confidence. When we're nervous, we have a tendency to speak faster and talk in a higher pitch. A quivering voice and talking in a higher octave will convey fear and insecurity. Slower speech patterns and talking in a lower tone can be a benefit. It gives the impression that you're strong and determined.

Speaking in a monotone is deadly dull and will only result in putting your interviewer to sleep. Emphasize key points by adding inflections to your voice. Practice varying your speech pattern and pitch before your interview. It will add more interest to the topics you're discussing and help keep your listener engaged.

WK *A S-I-M-P-L-E Idea:*

Practice varying your speech pattern and pitch before your interview. It will engage your listener and help add more interest to your topics. You may consider taping yourself with a tape recorder. When playing it back, evaluate your rate of speech and your tone of voice.

Matching Rates

Another more difficult method used to help build rapport is matching your speaking rate with that of your interviewer. We suggested earlier that you may want to slow down your rate of speech, but here is a situation where it may end up being a disadvantage. If your interviewer speaks at a faster rate, while you speak at a slower rate, it will make them impatient and put you out of sync. In this example, it would be better to match their faster rate of speech.

The opposite is also true. Speaking faster than your interviewer can make them feel you're in a rush and have something more important to do elsewhere. In this case, slowing down would be to your advantage and may help create a more compatible atmosphere.

As we mentioned earlier, mirroring is an incredibly valuable rapport builder. Matching another's speech rate and tone will only increase the bond you've been creating.

Summary

Things to remember:

- Always use good posture
- Keep your head level
- Never lower your head, eyes, or shoulders
- Develop a slower speech pattern
- Speak in a lower octave
- Vary your pitch to emphasize your point
- Match the speaking rate of your interviewer

7

POSITIVE AFFIRMATIONS

Many of you may be wondering why we included this topic in a book about body language. Affirmations are spoken statements that are a part of your *verbal* communication skills. This book is about *non-verbal* communications and gestures – so how do they relate? We've included this topic because thinking positively improves your confidence, which in turn improves your posture, puts a smile on your face, causes you to speak with more authority, and so on and so on. In essence, it has a direct impact on our non-verbal movements or gestures and indeed needs to be addressed in this book.

What Are Positive Affirmations?

Positive affirmations are statements we use to instill confidence or overcome negative thoughts. When we're stressed, our brains tend to dwell on the negative. Studies have shown that people who use positive affirmations can change their thought process and begin to create a better or more positive state of mind.

Create Optimism

Research has shown that people who are optimistic have many advantages. They usually have better health, tend to live longer, have better relationships with their spouses and co-workers, and manage or handle the stress in their lives much better. These are wonderful incentives for leading a positive lifestyle. Using affirmations to help achieve that positive lifestyle is an easy process and only takes a few minutes each day.

Since job interviewing can be a very stressful experience, we have come up with a few affirmations you may want to consider using prior to your interview. Practice each one first and see what feels right. Find the one that helps relieve stress, instill confidence, and in general, makes you feel better. That's the whole point - creating a better-feeling *you*.

Try these affirmations, or write some of your own:

- "This challenge brings me a great opportunity"
- "Today I have limitless possibilities"
- "I am strong, prepared, and ready to ace this interview"
- "All stress is leaving my body and I'm filled with positive energy"
- "I can stay calm under pressure"

Prior to your interview, while you're still in the car, take an opportunity to relieve some stress. First begin by trying to relax your face and body. Start by working from the top of your head to your face, neck, spine, then towards your waist and down your legs. Strive to relax each part of your body to relieve stored tension.

Once you're relaxed, begin to repeat your favorite affirmation statements. It's best to repeat them at least three times. Your brain responds best to messages repeated in threes. Once you have completed this process, you will find that your mind is relaxed and more confident and you're ready to present yourself for a great interview.

Acupressure or Pressure Point

Developed in China over 5,000 years ago, the manipulation of certain points on the body was said to help treat or relieve specific medical ailments. Though not used in the same manner in modern times, we can find benefit in using pressure points to relieve tension or make us more alert. Just like a nice massage helps us relax, the manipulation of a pressure point can also make us more attentive.

The pressure point between your index finger and your thumb can be very effective in increasing your alertness. This pressure point is at the base or "V" created between these two fingers. Apply firm and direct pressure at the muscle between the fingers and hold for 30 seconds. Then squeeze the same area on the other hand, again holding for 30 seconds.

Try this before each of your interviews to help increase your attentiveness and put you in a positive state of mind.

Summary

Things to do:

- Prepare in the car before your interview
- De-stress and relax your body
- Repeat your affirmations three times
- Think only positive thoughts
- Use acupressure to increase attentiveness
- Ace your interview

8

BE PREPARED

It's important that your body language exudes confidence during your interview. Most people respond positively to individuals who act self-assured. But your confidence can be broken if you go into your interview unprepared. Getting as much information about the company and how the interview will be conducted can give you that extra edge and help you remain poised during the process. Doing your homework beforehand will take some un-certainty out of your meeting and help assure that your body language will not betray you during a critical part of the inter-view.

Know Yourself

Nothing makes you look more ill-prepared than not knowing what information you have on your own resume or cover letter. You'd be surprised how many times candidates are caught off guard on a question that's directly related to an item on their resume. This can happen in several ways. One, your resume was prepared by someone else or two, you didn't review and remind yourself about the information concerning your past employment.

Your interviewer is using your resume as a road map and most likely will ask questions based upon information contained in the document. Review each line of your resume and cover letter. Anticipate any questions that can be implied about your employment history. Be prepared to expand in more depth on each item. It's best to show you are the expert concerning your own accomplishments. This is a sales presentation, and you are the product. Make sure you're always marketing yourself in the best possible light. Be specific in examples of your qualifications.

Know the Company

Have you ever been called by the wrong name? Even if it was an innocent mistake you end up feeling a bit slighted. Calling the company by an incorrect name or referring to the job by a wrong description shows your lack of preparedness. If you are doing several interviews in a short time, it's not unrealistic for this mistake to happen. Review all documents or information you have about this job before your interview. If you make a mistake, own up to it, identify it and immediately apologize for your error. The interviewer will be aware that it happened and pretending it didn't would be a mistake.

S-I-M-P-L-E Strategies in Action

"Know the Right Name" – *Submitted by Cheryl Phelps*

When interviewing for a journalist position, I inadvertently called the *Glenwood Post* the *Denver Post*. Unfortunately, the editor of the Glenwood Post was on the interview panel. I did eventually get the job, but it took this editor almost two years to respect me.

Find out all you can about the company and the position for which you're applying. Being able to show how a quality you possess can directly relate to a specific item or function for the company can be a feather in your cap.

You can do this by reading trade magazines, doing research on the internet, and even calling the company and talking with the receptionist. Let the receptionist know you are interviewing for a position with the company and you're interested in gathering some additional information. Ask them if they can take a moment to answer a few of your questions. Be prepared to ask a few pointed questions. Don't ask, "So what can you tell me about company ABC?" This person is busy and has a job to perform. Many times they will be willing to help answer a few questions, but don't make them do your homework. Thank the person before hanging up and make sure you show your appreciation again when you arrive for the interview. As we said earlier, you are always marketing yourself.

Expect the Unexpected

Depending upon the job, the interviewer may want to put you under some stress to see how well you can handle it. This is where your body language will play a big part.

Not displaying signs of aggravation, frustration or helplessness will assist you in showing you can handle the pressure. Try and anticipate these unexpected opportunities. Practice your body language with a friend or relative and have them ask you provoking questions.

Signs of Frustration

Also know your limitations or preferences. If long hours or traveling aren't what you want in a job, make sure you've thought this out before your interview. Again, you don't want to seem surprised when you're asked if traveling several weeks per month is an issue.

Types of Interviews

Another thing to prepare for to help you keep that confident and positive body language is to inquire what type of interview it will be. There are several different styles out there, and it would be in your best interest to become somewhat familiar with each type. Here are just a few, but you'll want to do more research.

54

➢ Telephone Interview: This is a common form of interview for initial screening. One trick you may want to consider is looking into a mirror as you conduct the interview. Watch your body language and smile. If you look happy and up-beat it will come across over the phone.

➢ One-on-One Interview: This is the traditional type of interview where the interviewer will have a full view of your body language reactions during the process.

➢ Panel Interviews: This becomes more complex since there are several people asking you questions. Trying to mirror or pace all the people on the panel can make you seem a bit peculiar. In this type of interview, it's better to focus on one or two members and work on them with your mirroring and eye contact.

➢ Group Interviews: This is where more than one candidate is being interviewed at the same time. Your confident and positive body language will give you a big boost and will make you stand out compared to the others.

➢ Stress Interviews: We talked about this one earlier. This type of interviewing process is meant to be trying and difficult. If needed, silently repeat your positive affirmation during breaks in the interview. This will help you keep that confident poise.

> Behavioral Interviews: In this process, the interviewer uses your past behaviors to indicate how you will react to future situations. You'll be asked questions to test your problem solving, adaptability, leadership, multi-tasking, and conflict resolution skills.

> Meandering Interviews: Many inexperienced interviewers may use this style. Here is where you most likely come upon the, "tell me about yourself" or "what did you do in your last job" questions. This is a great opportunity for you to take over the interview and direct the discussions to areas that best show your capabilities. Though you may have more control over this process, never try to dominate or show any disrespect.

Trying to anticipate what may happen will give you a better chance to appear confident and give you an edge.

WK *A S-I-M-P-L-E Idea:*

Prepare for the dreaded, "tell me about yourself" question. You don't want to try and wing this one. Here's an opening for you to do your best selling. Write it out and practice it several times. Make sure it describes your best attributes but doesn't come off as an egotistical elaboration.

S-I-M-P-L-E Strategies in Action

"Baby at 15" — *Submitted by Charlie Martin*

One of the things that I often enquire of prospective employees irrespective of the position they are applying is "What would you consider to be one of your greatest accomplishments?" I leave it up to them to decide whether to offer a professional or personal accomplishment.

I was somewhat surprised and indeed bewildered when the 20-something prospective employee responded to the question with "I had a baby at age 15." My first inclination was to say "wow-now that takes talent!" As much as her response should have been a red flag to me, the remainder of the interview went fairly well and I eventually hired the girl. After working here for several months I thought that her greatest accomplishment in life might someday be that she maintained the same job for more than a year, which in this case she failed.

Summary

Things to remember:

- Know your resume
- Keep the company name clear
- Understand the position for which you're applying
- Do your homework
- Talk with the receptionist beforehand
- Expect the unexpected
- Understand the different types of interviews

9

CHANGING THE SCENE

It's mid-way through your interview and you feel that things are not going as well as you'd hoped. You've prepared effectively. You've taken the time to check your appearance and attire. Your hair is styled, your fingernails are trimmed and looking neat. Your shoes are shined and your clothes are clean and well fitted. You have initiated a proper handshake and have actively participated in the interview process. But still you're not getting positive body responses from your interviewer. What can you do now?

It may be time to change the rhythm of the discussion. A change of mood may possibly change the energy between you and your interviewer. Before all is lost, you may want to consider changing the feel of the interview by doing one or more of the following.

Change Your Position

All during the interview, you've been mirroring the body position of your interviewer as we've suggested earlier. You've crossed or uncrossed your legs or held your arms and head in a reflective position. If this has not been working and you're still lacking rapport, it may be time to create change by sending out a non-verbal disruption. This disruption is effective because it catches the interviewer off guard and creates an emotional shock. This heightens their curiosity and gives you another opportunity to bring more interest to yourself and your abilities.

This change is subtle, but not subtle in effect. You can do this by abruptly changing your physical position, from a mirrored response, to something completely opposite. Breaking the mirrored effect, which you had been actively manufacturing throughout the process, will generate a disruptive force. If your interviewer is sitting with their legs crossed and body position facing towards the door, break this reflection by moving your legs into an open position and angling your body in the opposite direction.

Changing your position quickly is the key. This is not something you do slowly. This is a maneuver you do abruptly, forcefully, and all at once. However you must do it as though it is perfectly natural and not something that would seem crazy or threatening. Once you have renewed the attention of your interviewer, be ready to emphasize an interesting or key point of your background or abilities.

Vary Your Tone and Speed

We talked earlier about varying the tone of your voice while you speak. If you feel a lull is beginning, you may not want to do something drastic at this point, but you need to create a small shift in the atmosphere. Create a subtle change. You can easily do this by using more inflection in your voice and changing the speed of your vocal responses by talking a bit faster. These minor changes in your voice can add more interest and liven up the mood.

Bigger Gestures

Another tactic for changing the energy and interest level associated with your interview is to increase your physical gestures. While your gestures need to continue to be positive with open hands and upright palms, we want you to increase the size of your movements.

**Palms Up
Hands Open**

Refrain from making any wild motions, but extend your gestures a few more inches than you may currently be exhibiting. You may want to consider going just beyond the core of your body, but just by a few inches. Wild, flamboyant hand and arm gestures will make you look erratic, unstable, and a little crazed. This image will not win you any points with your interviewer, so keep the arm gestures somewhat contained.

61

Move or Remove

Another way to emphasize an important point is to remove your glasses (if you're wearing them), or move an item that's within your reach, especially if it's in front of you. These items create barriers, and barriers create a perceived distance between you and the interviewer. Removing or moving them out of the way promotes a feeling of being closer to the person you're speaking with and will once again create a stronger bond.

Use Props

Though we don't recommend this often, using props to highlight a point does have its advantages. Holding a pen, glasses, or a tablet in your hand as you're making gestures can accent your points. Never use them to point directly at your interviewer. This can be interpreted as a threatening movement.

Only use props on an occasional basis. Consider using them to emphasize an important point or if you need to change the mood. People tend to follow the prop with their eyes. Using them excessively or wildly can be distracting for the interviewer. Also, never use more than one prop, since your listener will not know which one to follow and this may create confusion.

Conclusion

Using props can add to your presentation or they can be a determent. Be very judicious in their use and employ sparingly.

S-I-M-P-L-E Strategies in Action

"*False* Confidence" – *Submitted by Lin McJunkin*

When I was in graduate school at UCLA, the student newspaper often carried ads from local agencies that were looking for models. One day, my boyfriend convinced me to apply for a job as a swimsuit model for a sailboat photo shoot.

While I had the requisite long blond hair and long tan legs, I was inadequately endowed for the upper area of any bikini. In those days before seemingly mandatory breast enhancement surgery, my boyfriend convinced me just to add some padding to my suit.

I went to the interview and shakily modeled for a room full of business-suited men. When I returned to the dressing room, I realized that my padding had slipped and was in full view at the edge of one bra cup.

I was mortified, but to their credit, not one man had snickered or betrayed the evidence of my secret assistant in any way. I didn't get the gig, but the next time I applied for a modeling job, I made sure any secret props were well hidden.

Summary

If you need to change the mood:

- Adjust your body position – move out of your mirroring position
- Change your angles
- Vary your vocal tones

Summary *(Continued)*

- Increase the speed of your speech
- Use bigger gestures
- Move or remove barriers to emphasize a point
- Use props, but sparingly

10

HOW DID YOU DO?

At the end of your interview you may have a reasonable idea about how well it went, but many times these impressions can be deceiving. You may think you did well, but in fact you didn't. Or the opposite may be true. Wouldn't it be great if you could read minds?

Well you can't read minds, of course, but you may be able to get a better understanding of what your interviewer is thinking by asking a few simple questions. In most interviews, you're expected to ask questions. You'll want to ask the obligatory questions concerning the company, the position, what's expected from you, and what you can expect from the company. Additionally, you'll want to ask questions that will generate specific responses from your interviewer. These responses will give you more insight into how well you performed during the interview, as well as whether or not they consider you a potential candidate for the position. The responses you're looking for will be both verbal and non-verbal. Let's take at look at both and see which signs will give us more information.

What to Ask

These questions must be thought provoking. Asking a general question such as, "Will I be a good candidate for the position?" will not generate the type of reactions that will lead to valuable insights. This type of question can be easily answered with a standard response. You want questions that will force the interviewer to do an evaluation and think of an appropriate response. This will induce a verbal and/or a non-verbal response that will show their true feelings.

Here are some examples of some thought-provoking questions:

- What aspects of my resume do you feel make me a good candidate for this position?
- Which accomplishments of mine would be of value to this company?
- What actions have I taken in the past that make me a valuable asset for this position?

Verbal Responses

As the interviewer responds to your question, listen for the use of pronouns such as "I," "we," or "us" in their response. When people are confident in what they're saying, they're more likely to use a pronoun. When they're not confident or trying to distance themselves from their comments, they'll show lack of commitment to their answers.

For example, if your interviewer was to respond to your question about; "which aspects of my resume make me a good candidate for this position?", and they use a pronoun such as, *"I like that you have 10 years of sales experience,"* you can feel comfortable in believing that this is a true statement and you're in the running for the job. On the other hand, if they respond by saying, *"You have several qualities that make you a good candidate,"* you might not have made a good impression or your specific skills are not in line with the qualifications for the position.

Here's another example: you ask, "Which accomplishments of mine would be of value to this company?" If your interviewer responds, *"We feel your past leadership skills would be valuable in this position,"* you can assume that you presented yourself well and you're a potential candidate. Again, a distancing response which lacks the use of a pronoun such as "I", "we", or "us" might mean trouble.

S-I-M-P-L-E Strategies in Action

"Mac 'n' Cheese" — *Submitted by Lizz Pellet*

After the warm greeting and cup of coffee or ice cold bottled water, the inquisition begins... "Are you a team player?" "What order were you picked for kickball on the playground?" "Do you have a pet and if so, what kind?" "If you had to eat one crayon in the box, what color would you eat and why?" asks a 20-something, popping her gum.

"Umm...the box of standard eight colors or can it be out of the box of 96 – you know the one with the sharpener in the back?" I ask. "Yeah, the box of 96 is fine I guess, but you can't pick that new color, Macaroni and Cheese, because that's like cheating," she says, her eyes narrowing at me.

67

The Non-Verbal Response

Non-verbal responses can be a bit more difficult to interpret. Keep your eyes open for the following responses. One obvious response is when the interviewer begins searching your resume to find an answer to accommodate your question. If you ask, "What actions have I taken in the past that make me a valuable asset for this position?", and the interviewer must look over your resume for an answer, you can assume that there was nothing during the interview that made a discernable impression on the interviewer concerning this aspect.

Other non-verbal cues may include the use of certain gestures and the use of or the lack of eye contact. When someone responds to your question with steady or continuous eye contact, this is a positive response and indicates that the interviewer is giving you an honest answer. The lack of eye contact during a response, however, shows the person doesn't believe what they're saying. Saying, *"You have a lot of good qualities,"* with no eye contact and the use of distance phrasing would lead you to believe they don't believe their own words.

Look not only for the lack of eye contact, but also for other gestures such as a smirk, lack of a smile, raised eyebrows, hands in a closed/fist position, and feet pointed away from you. If their feet are pointed toward the door, this would indicate they feel the interview is over and they want to leave. All these can be viewed as negative gestures. If displayed, these gestures show that the interviewer is uncomfortable making a response, mainly because most people don't enjoy giving others bad news.

When to Call Back

You don't want to be annoying, but waiting for the phone to ring can be a tremendous waste of your time. At the end of each interview ask if it would be appropriate to follow-up with a phone call after one week. Then if you haven't heard back from them, you have a convenient excuse to call. This will also help keep your name fresh in the recruiter's mind.

During the call make sure to reiterate your key qualifications and that you are still very interested in the position. Find out when a final decision (for the position) will be made. Ask if you can follow-up with another call after a reasonable time. Always try to leave yourself in a position to make additional calls without seeming over-bearing.

The ability to make follow-up calls will give you a small measure of control in the process. It will help relieve some of the anxiety while waiting for their call or guessing when it would be appropriate to call them.

Continue to Search

Even if the interview went well, continue to apply and interview for additional positions. You never want to leave all your eggs in one basket. You never know, you may find and even better position or find yourself in the enviable position of having to decide between more than one offer.

Summary

How well did you interview:

- Ask thought-provoking questions
- Listen for the use of pronouns in their answers (I, we, or us)

Summary *(Continued)*

- Look for positive or negative physical gestures
- Ask to do a follow-up call
- Continue looking

11

GOOD ENDINGS

A "Good" Good-Bye

Well, the interview is finally over. You breathe a big sigh of relief – but don't let the interviewer see it! With a warm smile, thank the interviewer for their time, shake hands good-bye, and leave the room with the same positive, confident body language you used to enter.

Even if you thought it was the interview from hell, leave with your head held high, showing nothing but grace and class to all you encounter. The interview isn't over until you've left the property, so don't break character until you're well away. If you need to vent, wait until you get home.

S-I-M-P-L-E Strategies in Action

"It's Not Over Until You're Gone" –
Submitted by Patti Lovetro-Clarke

I owned an espresso café for 12 years and people of all ages would apply regularly. More than once a young person would come in to apply with purple hair, nose rings, lip rings, tattoos, a t-shirt that didn't cover their midriff, jeans that showed their underwear and sit during the interview hunched over. After applying for a job they would sometimes sit on my patio with friends and proceed to smoke, spit, and use profane language while in front of my store. You have to be amused.

However, if you followed the advice contained within this book, it's likely your interview went off without a hitch. Studies show that job-hires who are well liked by the interviewer are more likely to land the job than others who may even be more qualified. We all want to work with people we like – it's human nature and that will never change. If your interviewer *likes* you, you'll have a better chance of being hired.

Touch in the Workplace

Though it's completely inappropriate to touch your interviewer other than your handshake both at the beginning and the end of your interview, you can strive to make your handshake really count. You may want to review our handshake discussion in Chapter 3.

Good Endings

As you prepare to leave at the conclusion of your interview, say something positive to your interviewer as you shake their hand. Make eye contact, smile, and be sure your hands are touching when you make the statement. Touch, during a positive moment, will increase your interviewer's good feelings toward you.

And what will make them feel good about you, is if *you* make them feel good about themselves. If you can, comment on something nice they did for you during the interview. If you're stuck, you may say something to the effect of "thank you for making me feel so welcome today. I really appreciate it."

Though we've cautioned you against touching your interviewer, it's perfectly okay if your hand brushes theirs as you accept the pen they hand you, or the glass of water they offer. Don't freak out if you touch them in this manner. In fact, it may work to your advantage. Appropriate touching bonds human beings together. Even an accidental touch of the hand or a quick, light touch on the forearm can do wonders for creating rapport. But at this point of the interview process, we would suggest being very careful about touch.

Now, once the interview is over and you've left the office, there's still more to do.

When you get home, sit down immediately and hand write a thank you note to your interviewer. Do not, we repeat do NOT send an email. The hand-written thank you note is fast becoming a lost art. But we guarantee you that your interviewer will be impressed by the time and effort you spent in writing a lovely, well-expressed note. This simple gesture may well be the very thing that tips the scale in your favor. NEVER underestimate the power of a hand-written note!

Sample Letter

If writing a thank you note fills you with dread, you're not alone. Many people struggle to find the right words to say. Here are some simple guidelines to follow which may help you make your "thank you" seem more sincere.

- Say "thank you" at least twice – once at the beginning and once at the end.

- Acknowledge any special treatment you may have received.

- Highlight your qualities once again, but in a general way (you already had a chance to "sell" yourself during the interview. However, if you forgot something critical, briefly explain, and then move on).

- Add something a little more personal (without overstepping appropriate boundaries), such as commenting on something you two may have discussed about your families, sports, favorite restaurants, etc.

- Sign with your whole name, not just your first name.

Following is a sample you may feel free to use to give you a head start on your own thank you notes:

Dear Mr./Mrs./Ms. (and interviewer's last name):

I'd like to thank you once again for taking the time to meet with me today for our interview at the ABC Company. I know you had a very busy schedule, which made all the time and energy you spent with me that much more appreciated. I sincerely value all the advice and input you gave me as to how I might improve my resume, and I will put your suggestions to good use. You were very kind to help me that way.

I would be honored to become part of the ABC family and feel that my experience, values, and commitment would be a great asset to the company. It is my hope that you feel the same way. If there is any further information you may require from me, please don't hesitate to ask. Thank you once again for all your help.

P.S. I hope your son's Little League team won their game!

Sincerely,

Your Name

Everyone likes to be appreciated for the things they do to help others. Make your interviewer feel special by pointing out how grateful you are for any extra attention you received, such as the help they gave you with your resume. The interviewer knows that they're there to learn about *you*, but by mentioning some personal detail the two of you may have shared (such as their son's baseball game) it shows that you were interested in them too, and they may think more fondly of you as a result. It will also show that you pay attention to details.

It's important to be sincere in your note. Fawning, gushing, and fake flattery will be easily spotted and any value that could be achieved by hand writing a note will be lost.

If your handwriting is atrocious, we have only one word for you. Print. If your printing is horrible too, you're going to need to practice, practice, practice. Poor handwriting skills are not going to win you any points at a job interview, so practice!

First, write or type your note on another piece of paper and get all the wording just right. Then, when you're ready, take your time and carefully write or print the note onto a card or piece of stationery. Mail the note right away and then sit back and wait to hear you got the job!

Summary

Keep it positive to the very end:

- Arrive with confidence and leave with confidence
- Avoid inappropriate touching
- Wait until you're off company property to relax
- As soon as you get home, compose a thank you letter to your interviewer
- Make the letter sincere and hand write it – no emails!
- If you have bad handwriting, practice!
- Mail it right away
- Relax, you've done a great job!

Epilogue

Our hope is that you'll use this book to improve your body language skills as you prepare for your next job interview. Remember, the majority of information you communicate to your interviewer will be *non-verbal*. Understanding how your gestures and facial expressions are perceived, and how to interpret them in others, will give you more tools than the average person and put you in an advantageous position.

We always like to hear how the skills we've taught you have helped you in your quest for a new job. Please take the opportunity to email us with your stories and experiences. You may find one of your stories in our blog or on our website.

If you're interested in learning more, check out our website for new tricks and tips as well as the schedule for our popular training seminars. We may be coming to your area soon.

We wish you the best of luck in your next job interview. It's one of the hardest processes you will go through in life. Hopefully we've made it a bit more comfortable and easy for you. Take care and good luck. – *Michael Willson and Karen Kelly*

Willson-Kelly Presentations

Willson-Kelly
"Workshops & Seminars"

Visit our website or email us to find out our current schedule for our popular *"Body Language"* workshops.

Mike and Karen provide keynote addresses, seminars and breakout sessions for corporate clients, trade associations and government agencies. Contact us at:

Website: www.willson-kelly.com

Email Address: wkpresentations@yahoo.com

Bibliography

Andersen, Peter A. Ph.D, *The Complete Idiot's Guide to Body Language*. New York: The Penguin Group USA.

Axtell, Roger E. *Essential Do's and Taboos: The Complete Guide to International Business and Leisure Travel*. Hoboken, New Jersey: John Wiley & Sons, Inc.

Buckingham, Marcus and Donald O. Clifton, Ph.D. *Now Discover Your Strengths*. New York: The Free Press.

Carnegie, Dale. *How to Win Friends & Influence People*. New York: Pocket Books, a Division of Simon & Schuster Inc.

Cialdini, Robert B. Ph.D. *The Psychology Influence of Persuasion*. New York: Harper Collins Publisher

Cohen, Steve. *Win the Crowd*. New York: Harper Collins Publisher

Davis, Martha, Ph.D, Elizabeth Robbins Eshelman, MSW, Matthew McKay, Ph.D. *The Relaxation & Stress Reduction Workbook*. Oakland, California: New Harbinger Publications

Goman, Carol Kinsey. *The Nonverbal Advantage: Secrets and Science of Body Language at Work*. San Francisco, California: Berrett-Koehler Publisher, Inc.

Bibliography

Hill, Napoleon. *Think and Grow Rich*. San Diego, California: Avetine Press, Inc.

Henley, Nancy M. *Body Politics: Power, Sex & Nonverbal Communication*. New York: Published by Simon & Schuster Inc.

Hogan, Kevin. *The Science of Influence: How to Get Anyone to Say "Yes" in 8 Minutes or Less*. Hoboken, New Jersey: John Wiley & Sons, Inc.

Hogan, Kevin and James Speakman. *Covet Persuasion: Psychological Tactics and Tricks to Win the Game*. Hoboken, New Jersey: John Wiley & Sons, Inc.

Kraus, Stephen J. Ph.D. *Psychological Foundations of Success: A Harvard-Trained Scientist Separates the Science of Success from Self-Help Snake Oil*. San Francisco, California: Change-Planet Press.

Lieberman, David J. Ph.D *You Can Read Anyone*. New Jersey: Viter Press

Pease, Allan and Barbara Pease. *The Definitive Book of Body Language*. New York: Bantam Books

Quilliam, Susan. *Body Language: Learn to Read and Use the Body's Secret Signals*. New York: Firefly Books.

Reiman, Tonya. *The Power of Body Language*. New York: Pocket Books, a Division of Simon & Schuster Inc.

Sargent, Allen C. *The Other Mind's Eye: the gateway to the hidden treasures of your mind*. Malibu, California: Success Design International Publications

Weiss, Allan. *Money Talks: How to Make a Million as a Speaker*. McGraw-Hill

Williams, Patrick and Diane S. Menendez. *Becoming a Professional Life Coach*. New York: W.W. Norton & Company

Whitworth, Laura, Karen Kimsey-House, Henry Kimsey-House and Phillip Sandahl, *Co-Active Coaching: New Skills for Coaching People Towards Success in Work and Life*. Mountain View, California. Davies-Black Publishing

Interview Log

Date: _____

Company: _____

Position applying: _____

Sent thank you letter: Y / N   Date: _____

Follow-up call on: _____

Date: _____

Company: _____

Position applying: _____

Sent thank you letter: Y / N   Date: _____

Follow-up call on: _____

Date: _____

Company: _____

Position applying: _____

Sent thank you letter: Y / N   Date: _____

Follow-up call on: _____

(Continued Next Page)

Interview Log

(Continued)

Date: _____

Company: _____

Position applying: _____

Sent thank you letter: Y / N   Date: _____

Follow-up call on: _____

Date: _____

Company: _____

Position applying: _____

Sent thank you letter: Y / N   Date: _____

Follow-up call on: _____

Date: _____

Company: _____

Position applying: _____

Sent thank you letter: Y / N   Date: _____

Follow-up call on: _____